What on Earth?
Life in the Desert

What on Earth?

What a scorcher!

The hottest desert in the world is the Sahara in Africa. At the hottest point in the day the sand is so hot it can burn through the skin on the soles of your feet in seconds.

So how does anything survive in a desert?

Find out in this book.

Published in 2005 in the United States by Children's Press,
an imprint of Scholastic Library Publishing,
90 Sherman Turnpike, Danbury, CT 06816

ISBN 0-516-25317-4 (Lib. Bdg.)

A CIP catalog record for this title is available from the Library of Congress.

Printed and bound in China.

Editor:	Ronald Coleman
Senior Art Editor:	Carolyn Franklin
DTP Designer:	Mark Williams

Picture Credits Julian Baker: 2, 3, 6, 7, 8(t), 9, 16, 19(t),
24(t), Elizabeth Branch: 8(b), 9(b), Mark Bergin: 19(b),
24(b), A.N.T Photo Library: 20(b), Mike Lane, NHPA: 21,
Free Agents LTD, Corbis: 25(b), Digital Vision: 10, 11, 12,
13, 14, 15, 17, 22, 23, 25(t), 27, 31, PhotoDisc: 18, 28,
PhotoSpin.com: 20(t), John Foxx: 26, 29

Cover © 2005 Rod Patterson/Gallo Images/Corbis Images

What on Earth?

Tricky toads

When caught in a predator's
mouth, a horny toad squirts
blood. This tastes so bad
that the toad is dropped,
giving it a chance to escape.

What on Earth?

Life in the Desert

GERALD LEGG

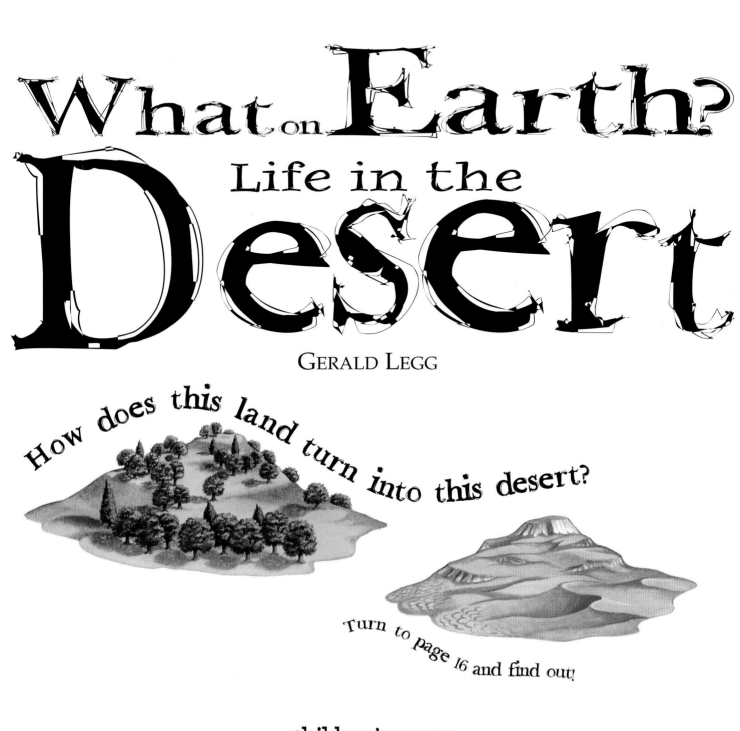

How does this land turn into this desert?

Turn to page 16 and find out!

children's press®

A Division of Scholastic Inc.

NEW YORK • TORONTO • LONDON • AUCKLAND • SYDNEY

MEXICO CITY • NEW DELHI • HONG KONG

DANBURY, CONNECTICUT

Contents

What on Earth?

Desert tricks?

In a hot desert, desperate travelers can be fooled into thinking they see an oasis. As they rush towards it, it vanishes. This is called a mirage. It is a trick of the light.

Introduction

A desert is defined as land with less than 10 inches (25 centimeters) of rain a year. Many hot deserts have no rain at all for years. Some deserts only have fogs and heavy dews. Desert days are very hot but the nights are very cold! It is not just heat that dries the desert but it is also the wind. Strong winds from the Sahara Desert in North Africa can blow sand as far away as Italy.

Is there ever water in the desert?

Most desert rain falls during very violent thunderstorms. Riverbeds that have been dry and cracked fill with water quickly and can overflow and cause mudslides and flooding.

What happens when the storm is over?

Seeds and plant roots that have been waiting for rain now burst into life filling the desert with flowers and insects. They must complete their lifecycles quickly, forming seeds and laying eggs before the desert is too hot and dry again.

What Is a Desert?

Imagine a desert. What do you see — nothing but sand with a baking hot sun overhead? No. Not all deserts are hot. Some are always cold like the desert on Antarctica around the South Pole. There the sun is never overhead, and the desert is too cold for anything to grow. So how can deserts be in very **hot** regions and very **cold** regions? Deserts, whether hot or cold, are always very **dry** places.

Animals in hot deserts usually rest until night when it is cooler. To cope with the heat and lack of water, most desert animals do not sweat. Creatures like the kangaroo rat never drink. They get all their liquid from the food they eat.

Gila woodpecker

Coyote

Desert scorpion

Kit fox

Rattlesnake

Kangaroo rat

6

American kestrel

Saguaro cactus

Costa's hummingbird

Burrowing owl

Elf owl

Desert spiny lizard

Mule deer

Monarch butterfly

Jack rabbit

Spiny lizard

Gila monster

Where Are Deserts?

There are deserts on every continent on Earth. The Sahara Desert in Africa is the **largest** desert and covers almost as much land as the whole United States.

Canada

North America

Atlantic Ocean

Pacific Ocean

South America

Antarctica

Areas of desert around the world are shown on these two maps (*above*).

Jack rabbit

Chuckwalla

Sage grouse

North America has five main deserts. The best-known is the Painted Desert in Arizona. The other deserts are the Great Basin, the Sonoran, the Mojave and the Chichuahua Desert of Mexico.

Is Australia the driest continent?

Asia

Europe

Africa

Pacific Ocean

Indian Ocean

Australia

Antarctica

Antarctica is even drier than Australia. But Antarctica's desert is very cold and Australia's desert is very hot.

Which desert is the size of France?

Rub' al Khali is the largest desert in Saudi Arabia. It is known as the Empty Quarter because nothing lives there. It is about the size of France!

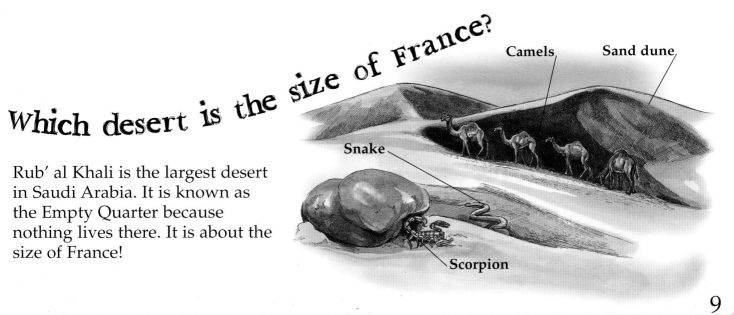

Camels

Sand dune

Snake

Scorpion

9

Are All Deserts Sandy?

Most deserts have sand but deserts also have large areas covered in gravel or rocks. Plants could not grow in deserts without stony areas. Why? Sand is always shifting in the desert winds, so plants have no time to put down roots and grow. Plants also need water, which would soak straight through sand.

Where does the rain go?

When rain soaks through the sand it reaches hard rock and it becomes an underground stream. These streams can bubble up in stony areas of the desert. Here brilliant green, leafy plants grow. The plants and water attract animals, insects, birds, and humans. This fertile area in a desert is called an oasis.

Some oases have been there for centuries. If an oasis dries up, the plants and trees die and people move on. Soon only the skeletons of trees remain.

The Namib Desert, in Africa.

What on Earth?

Rain, what's that?

Rain fell in the Atacama Desert in northern Chile in 1971. It had not rained there for **400 years!** The Atacama is one of the world's driest deserts.

Why Are Deserts Dry?

Deserts are dry because very little moisture reaches them. Wind blowing over warm seas picks up moisture which falls as rain when it reaches land. By the time wind reaches the center of a continent it has no moisture left and is dry.

Which desert is the size of Disney World?

The Navajo Nation's Monument Valley Park in Nevada, USA, covers an area as big as Disney World in Florida.

What is the skeleton coast?

The long narrow Namib Desert is on the Atlantic coast of southwest Africa. The desert's shores are known as The Skeleton Coast because so many ships were wrecked there.

What on Earth?

No sand?

Most of Antarctica is a desert, but there is no sand on that continent. Its climate is the coldest on Earth. It is called a desert because it's so dry.

Have There Always Been Deserts?

There have always been deserts on Earth but not always where they are now. Over millions of years the Earth's climate has gone through cycles of warm and cold periods which have changed its landscape. Archeologists have found the bones of woolly **mammoths** in southern England, yet they would only have lived in very cold places. So England must once have been much, much colder.

What is The Mexican Hat?

Sand dunes over 136 million years old now form the Cliffs of Zion in the Great Basin Desert in Nevada. Over time, rocks are worn away leaving strange shapes like The Mexican Hat.

Why Do the Rocks Look Like This?

These finger-like rocks in the Nambung National Park, Australia, are thousands of years old. The soft limestone rock has been worn away by the desert sand and wind.

What on Earth?

skyscrapers?

Windswept sand forms huge mounds called dunes. The highest known sand dunes are in Algeria, in the Sahara Desert. They are 508 yards (465 meters) high. The Empire State Building in New York is only 417 yards (381 meters) high!

Do Deserts Grow or Shrink?

 ver time deserts can grow or shrink. At this time more deserts are growing than shrinking. A desert will spread when vegetation at its edges is killed off by drought. Without vegetation to protect it, the soil is blown or washed away and the land becomes a desert.

How does land become a desert?

1.

Where there is rain and the soil is rich, plants and animals can live and grow. People settle in such places to work and farm.

2.

If forests are cut down and cleared for crops, grazing and firewood, the soil is left exposed to the sun and wind.

3.

The soil disappears, blown away by the wind or washed away in flash floods. If the land is overgrazed, only poor, scrubby plants can survive.

4.

Fires and strong winds cause damage that helps deserts to spread. If the rains fail and wells and springs run dry, the land can become a desert.

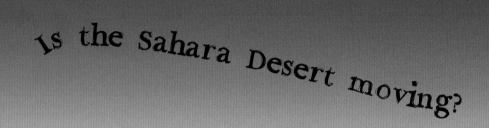

Is the Sahara Desert moving?

The area known as the Sahara Desert was not always a desert. A long time ago, the Sahara was rich farming land. It supplied the Roman Empire with most of its grain. In the last 50 years the Sahara Desert has grown by about two and a half miles (4 kilometers) a year.

What on Earth?

Buried city?

The Sahara's sand dunes are spreading towards Nouakchott, the capital city of Mauritania in Africa, and threaten to bury it.

Riches in the Desert?

Deserts are harsh places to live, but treasure may lie under them. The main treasure is oil. Like coal, oil forms over **millions** of years from the remains of plants and animals. This shows that areas that we now know as deserts were once covered in forests.

What on Earth?

Armored lizard?

The armadillo lizard's armored body gives it complete protection. When in danger it rolls itself up with its tail held tightly in its jaws to protect its soft belly.

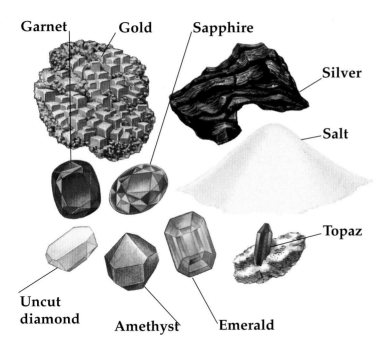

Garnet Gold Sapphire
Silver
Salt
Topaz
Uncut diamond
Amethyst Emerald

The desert is also rich in precious metals and gems, including copper, gold, silver, uranium and diamonds. Natural salts called gypsum and borates are processed and used in building materials, glass and pottery. Drug companies also make use of them.

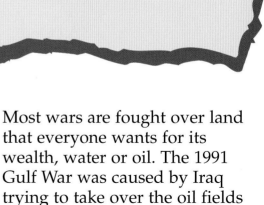

Most wars are fought over land that everyone wants for its wealth, water or oil. The 1991 Gulf War was caused by Iraq trying to take over the oil fields of Kuwait in the Arabian Desert.

Armored tank!

19

How Do Desert Animals Survive?

A desert animal's life is very hard. The heat and lack of water are its biggest problems. Most creatures shelter from the heat of the sun and appear only at night. Many burrow underground. They have had to adapt to survive in the desert.

Stinger in tail

Pincer

Scorpions detect the tiniest movements of their prey. They grab it with large pincer-like claws and inject a deadly venomous sting from the end of their tail.

Which lizard blows up like a balloon?

If the thorny skin of this thorny devil doesn't repel predators, it has another trick. It can blow itself up like a balloon when attacked.

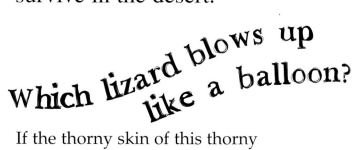

Thorny devil

What on Earth?

Why rattle?

The Eastern diamond-back is the largest rattlesnake at six and a half feet (2 meters) long. It shakes the tip of its tail (its rattle) to scare off enemies.

Many snakes hunt at night. They sense the body heat of their prey even in total darkness.

Ship of the desert?

Camels are called "ships of the desert" because they carry people and their belongings through the desert. They can travel for long distances without food or water. Like many desert animals they don't lose water by sweating. The dromedary camel has one hump and the bactrian camel has two humps.

Nostrils can be closed almost completely in a sandstorm.

Long eyelashes to protect its eyes from sand and sun.

The hump is full of fat, a built-in supply of fluid to nourish the camel over long distances.

Ears can flatten for protection in a sandstorm.

Thick knee pads for kneeling and resting.

Tough lips that can grip thorny plants.

A camel's stomach holds a huge amount of food and water. It can drink 30 gallons (114 liters) of water at one time. An average car holds 12 gallons of gasoline.

Long sturdy legs make camels good runners.

Wide, padded feet which splay out help to stop the camel from sinking into the sand.

How Do Plants survive in the Desert?

Plants have adapted to survive in the desert. Hairs and prickly spines protect plants like cacti from heat and stop animals from eating them. Desert plants have long roots to search out water and tough skins to stop moisture from escaping.

What on Earth?

Cactus fountain?

Cacti are only found in the deserts of North and South America. When a giant saguaro cactus is 33 feet (10 meters) tall, it can contain hundreds of gallons of liquid.

How long did this arm take to grow?

The giant saguaro cactus, found only in the Sonoran Desert in the USA, can live for up to 200 years. It takes between 75 to 100 years for one cactus arm to grow!

Giant saguaro cactus

Fridge or tree?

When a kokerboom tree dies people hollow out its trunk and use it to keep food fresh because it acts like a natural refrigerator. The kokerboom or quiver tree grows in Namibia in Africa. The Khoikhoi bushmen make arrow quivers from its branches.

23

How Do People Live in Deserts?

Deserts may be harsh, but people have lived in them for at least 300,000 years. Nomads are desert people who live in temporary tent-like structures. They move from place to place in search of food and water. Their clothes help them to stay cool and protect them from the wind-blown sand.

Mongolians in central Asia and Bedouins in Saudi Arabia are both nomadic tribes.

A Mongolian yurt

Yurts look more like portable huts than tents. Thick layers of felt are laid over a wooden frame.

Do Bedouins travel light?

The nomadic Bedouins of the Sahara Desert travel long distances with everything they own strapped on the backs of camels.

A Bedouin tent

Bedouins live in tents made of goats' hair cloth. They are light and easy to put up.

24

What on Earth?

Chilly nights brrr!

The Gobi Desert in Asia is bitterly cold at night. The temperature can fall to -40°F (-40°C).

Off-road vehicles driving in the desert destroy the sand dunes and fragile desert soils.

When did Aborigines reach Australia?

Aborigines reached the continent of Australia 50,000 to 60,000 years ago. Since then they have learned to live in harmony with its harsh climate. Their life is closely linked to the land, its animals, plants and the world of spirits. To the Aborigines, everything in the natural world is important and is worthy of respect.

What Are the Dangers in the Desert?

Deserts are dangerous places. Water is the key to survival. Your body can lose 8 cups of water in one hour! Your body also loses salt when you sweat. This weakens you and can cause cramps, confusion, and even death.

What on Earth?

Dust devils?

Run for cover!

Dust devils look like small tornadoes. They suck up sand and dust as they spin across the desert. These sand-filled columns of hot air can be half a mile (804 meters) high.

How would you survive in the desert?

Look for shade by day. Travel at night when it is cooler. Use the stars to help you find your way. Water is much more important than food in the desert. So take things slowly and do not waste your energy.

Desert dangers

Panicking If you are lost in the desert, panicking will only make the problem worse. Think calmly, consider your options and decide on a plan.

Sun stroke Early symptoms are panting and drooling. Loosen clothing, find shelter, and submerge yourself in cool water...if you can find any!

Rattlesnakes Although rattlesnakes try to avoid human contact they are very dangerous when provoked. Rattlesnakes kill over a dozen people in the USA every year. If bitten keep warm and call emergency services immediately.

What to take Checklist

A **hat** keeps the sun off your head and protects your neck from sunburn. **Sunglasses with** special dark lenses protect eyes from the glare of the sun. **Strong boots and thick socks** stop your feet from being rubbed by the sand. A **scarf** to protect your face from the sand, sun, and heat. A **loose long-sleeved shirt** and **long pants** made from sun-reflecting fabric. **Sunscreen** to help protect your skin. A **warm jacket** to keep warm at night.

Desert Facts

Desert sand grains are round, unlike water-worn sand grains found on beaches.

Avalanches don't only occur in snowy regions. If a sand dune collapses it is called an avalanche.

A sand dune avalanche can be heard as far as 6 miles (10 kilometers) away.

Walking across sand is not easy. Many desert rodents jump instead.

Cactus

The world's highest temperature, 136°F (58°C), was recorded in the Sahara Desert.

The Sahel region in Africa became a desert in the 1970's due to drought and over-farming.

A bactrian camel has a thick fur coat for warmth in the cold Gobi Desert. In the summer it sheds its fur and becomes almost hairless.

The Rub' al-Khali desert in southern Arabia is the longest area of continuous sand in the world.

The sand lizard of the Namib Desert lifts its legs up and down from the burning sand or lies on its stomach to cool all its feet at once.

Glossary

archeologist a person who studies earlier times from the remains that are left

Antarctica at the bottom of the globe, the continent of Antarctica is nearly covered with ice

continent one of Earth's main land masses

diamond very hard precious stone

dromedary camel with one hump

drought a long spell of very dry weather

erosion gradual wearing away of something

fertile land that is fertile is good for growing crops

moisture liquid

nomad someone who moves from place to place, usually in search of food for the herd of animals

overgrazed when too many animals graze on the same land for a long time, the ground becomes damaged

Hooded oriole (Male)

What Do You Know About the Desert?

1. What is the largest desert in the world?

2. What is the driest desert in the world called?

3. When is an area called a desert?

4. What valuable black liquid is found under some deserts?

5. What should you do to survive in a desert?

6. Why does a cactus have prickly spines?

7. What is the largest desert on Earth?

8. Why does a rattlesnake "rattle"?

9. What is in a camel's hump?

10. What is a mirage?

Go to page for 32 for the answers!

What is this rock called?

Go to page for 32 for the answer!

Index

Pictures are shown in **bold** type

Answers

1. The Sahara in North Africa (See page 8)
2. The Atacama Desert in northern Chile, South America (See page 11)
3. When a place has less than 10 inches (25 cm) of rain each year (See page 5)
4. Oil (See page 18)
5. Stay calm and cover your skin and head (See page 27)
6. To protect against heat and to stop animals from eating them (See page 22)
7. The Sahara Desert in Africa (See page 8)
8. To frighten enemies away (See page 20)
9. A store of fat (See page 21)
10. An illusion that makes distant objects appear much closer (See page 4)

The Devil's Marbles are a collection of gigantic round rocks. Some of them are precariously balanced on top of one another. Scattered heaps of these "marbles" occur across a wide, shallow valley north of Alice Springs, Australia.